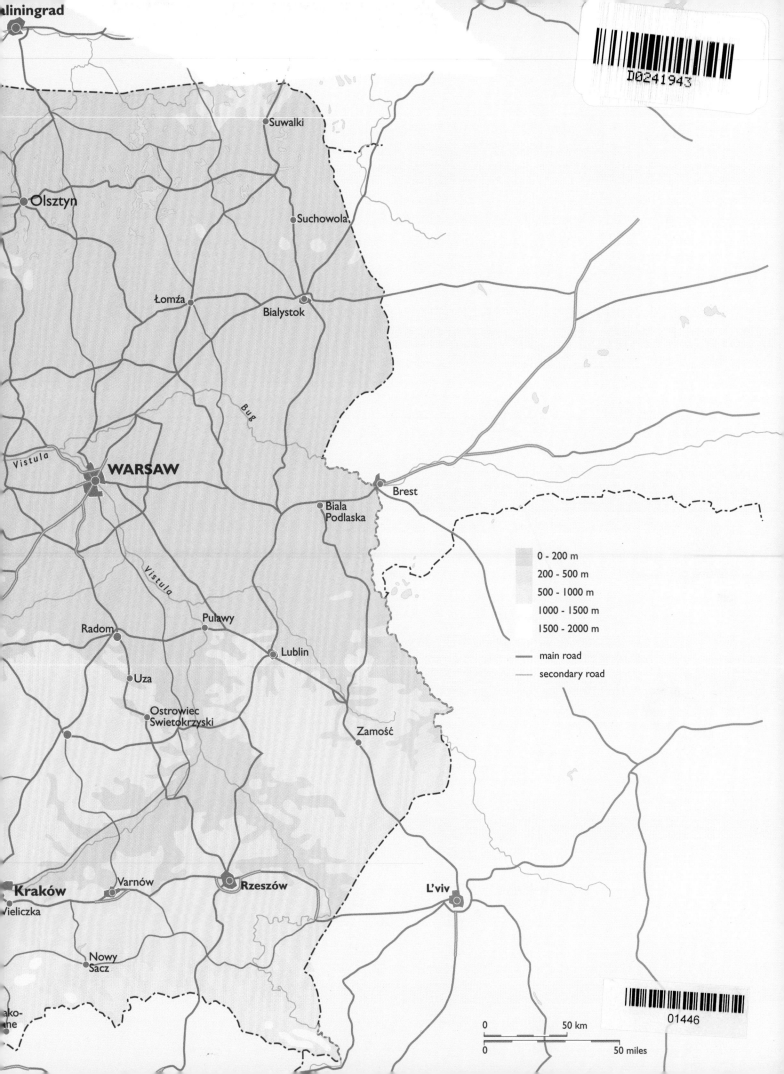

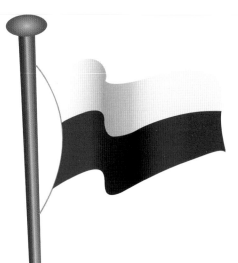

New EU Countries and Citizens

Poland

Jan Kądziołka
Tadeusz Wojciechowski

A Cherrytree Book

This edition published in 2006 by Evans Brothers Limited
Reprinted in 2009
2A Portman Mansions
Chiltern Street
London W1U 6NR, UK

Published by arrangement with KIT Publishers, The Netherlands

Copyright © 2004 KIT Publishers – Amsterdam

British Library Cataloguing-in-Publication Data
Kadziolka, Jan
Poland. - (New EU countries and citizens)
1. Poland - Juvenile literature
I. Title
II. Wojciechowski, Tadeusz
943.8
9781842343203

Text: Jan Kądziołka and Tadeusz Wojciechowski
Photographs: Jan Willem Bultje
Translation: Jeske Nelissen
UK editing: Sonya Newland
Design and Layout: Grafisch Ontwerpbureau Agaatsz BNO, Meppel, The Netherlands
Cover: Big Blu Ltd
Cartography: Armand Haye, Amsterdam, The Netherlands
Production: J & P Far East Productions, Soest, The Netherlands

Picture Credits
Photographs: Jan Willem Bultje
p. 8 (b), 16 (b), 21 (t) 25 (b), 28 (t), 29, 35 (b), 40 (b) , 41 (t), 42, 43 (t), 44, 45, 46 en 47: Polish
Tourist Organization; p.19 (t), 25 (t) Janek Skarzynski, p. 14(t) Stanislaxw Ciok, p. 38 (c), p.
39 (t) Piotr Krzyzannowsky Przemyslaw Pokrycki: Epa Photo; p. 22(b) © Raymond
Gehman/CORBIS; p. 27(b) © Paul Almasy/CORBIS; p. 30(t) © Raymond Gehman/CORBIS;
p. 37(t) © Raymond Gehman/CORBIS; p. 41(b) © Steve Raymer/CORBIS

Contents

4   Introduction

6   History

10 The country

14 Towns and cities

22 People and culture

26 Education

31 Cuisine

34 Transport

37 The economy

41 The environment

44 Nature and tourism

46 Poland in the EU

48 Glossary and index

Introduction

Poland is a fascinating country, filled with diverse landscapes – mountains, plains, rivers and forests – beautiful architecture and rich traditions. It also has a long and varied history, during which it has had periods of great prosperity and severe hardship.

Poland is one of the largest countries in Europe. To the north lies the Baltic Sea, but the rest of the country is surrounded by land – Germany and the Czech Republic to the west, Slovakia and Ukraine to the south, Belarus and Lithuania to the east and Kaliningrad, a region of Russia, to the north-east. The capital and largest city is Warsaw. Most of Poland is made up of lowlands, except the far south of the country, which is lined by the Carpathian and Sudeten Mountains. Across the lowland regions are many ancient lakes and forests, and a number of national parks and nature reserves have been established to protect the flora and fauna of the countryside.

Poland's almost-landlocked position in the middle of Europe has caused problems throughout its history, and at various points in the past Poland has fallen under the control of its neighbouring countries. This happened most recently at the beginning of the Second World War, when Germany

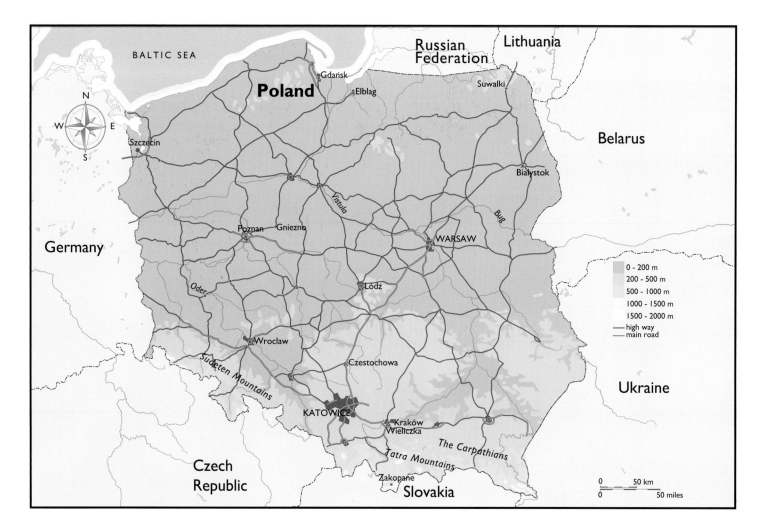

invaded Poland and occupied it for six years. Each time, however, the people have fought to regain their independence, and eventually succeeded. Perhaps because of this, the Poles have a strong sense of national identity and are proud of their traditions and beliefs.

In recent years Poland's fortunes have begun to rise. It is still not a wealthy country like those in Western Europe, but the government has introduced many reforms – including modernising industry, improving transport, and encouraging more trade with other countries. When Poland joined the European Union on 1 May 2004, it brought the country full circle in its relationship with western Europe.

▼ *The high street in Gdańsk, showing some of Poland's colourful architecture and thriving city life.*

▲ *The majority of Polish people are Roman Catholics, and one of the most famous Poles was the last pope, John Paul II.*

History

The territory that is now Poland was once home to various tribes that ventured there from neighbouring lands. By the ninth century AD, the Polian peoples had begun to rule the Slavs and the roots of the Polish nation were sown. The Polish state itself was established at the end of the tenth century by Mieszko I, a prince of a great Polish dynasty.

In the Middle Ages, Poland was a huge and powerful state – spanning almost one million square kilometres. The sixteenth century saw the height of Poland's greatness and this period became known as a golden age in the country's history. Art and culture flourished, and the people grew rich. Evidence of this can still be seen in some of the magnificent buildings that have survived in Poland. Many of these can be found in Krakow, which used to be the country's capital city. Among the most famous buildings are the Wawel Castle, where the Polish kings used to live, and the Mariacki Church (Church of the Virgin Mary).

▼ *The most striking features of the Mariacki Church in Krakow are the two towers. The taller tower (left) has a spire topped with a gold-plated crown.*

▲ *The market square in Krakow is the largest in Europe. It was designed in 1257, and although the buildings around it are more recent, they still have the original medieval cellars.*

This success was not to last, though. By the end of the eighteenth century, three of Poland's neighbouring countries – Russia, Prussia and Austria – had agreed to take over Poland and divide the land between them. This was known as the 'Partitions of Poland'. When the last Partition took place in 1795, the country completely lost its independence and the state of Poland ceased to exist.

Over the next few years, the people of Poland struggled for survival and freedom. They threw out a challenge to the rest of Europe, saying:

'Poland has not yet succumbed, as long as we remain. What the foe by force has seized, sword in hand we'll gain.'

These words – along with the folk tune called the *Mazurek* – became the national anthem.

In the Middle Ages, there were religious wars in several countries across Western Europe. Many people suffered and died for their beliefs, often being burnt at the stake. Throughout this time Poland was famous for its religious tolerance, and became known as 'the state without stakes'. Poland was also the first country in Europe (the second in the world after North America) to adopt its own democratic constitution, in 1791. Poland's history also shows that its people understood the benefits of international co-operation. As early as 1569, Poland established the Lublin Union with Lithuania, which joined 'the free with the free, the equal with the equal'. Under the terms of the union, Poland and Lithuania remained independent states but were joined by the alliance and the ruler. The state was called the 'Republic of Two Nations'.

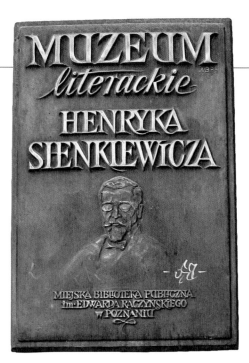

▲ The famous Polish writer Henryk Sienkiewicz won the Nobel Prize for Literature in 1905. He was born in the Russian part of Poland and his family took part in the struggles for independence.

▼ Conditions were difficult in Poland during the Second World War. More than six million Poles were killed and around 2.5 million more were sent to do forced labour in Germany.

Russia had gained the biggest part of Poland in the Partition, and so the Polish Legions fighting for the country's freedom focused on the Russian tsar. In November 1830 an uprising occurred in the city of Warsaw, which was occupied by the Russians. This was called the November Revolution and it lasted for a year. Initially the Poles managed to drive the Russians out of Warsaw, but by 1831 the city had been retaken and the Poles defeated.

Over the next few decades, uprisings occurred across Austrian and Prussian territories. The biggest and most tragic of these was the January Uprising, which began in 1863. During these rebellions, thousands of Poles perished on battlefields, or were executed by shooting or hanging. Even more Poles died in prisons and in the freezing and inhumane conditions of Siberia, where they were deported.

After the uprisings were suppressed, emigration started. Thousands of Poles went into exile to escape the harsh conditions of life under occupation. Even though they had been defeated, the Polish people tried to keep their national identity. They did this by continuing to speak their own language and by maintaining their own traditions and beliefs.

The First World War

In 1914 the First World War broke out. Because the countries responsible for the Partitions stood against each other in this new conflict, the Poles realised that their enemies were weaker than they

◀ Veterans who fought in the Polish army against the German occupation still have annual memorial gatherings.

▼ A statue of Józef Piłsudski in Łódź. Piłsudski was briefly imprisoned, but when Poland gained independence in 1918 he returned to lead his country.

had been. They saw an opportunity to strike back – perhaps they could win their independence after many years of occupation.

The Polish Legions – organised by the independence movement activist and future leader of the nation Józef Piłsudski – initiated the fight against Russia. Polish divisions that had formed in France also followed him. Other countries began to pay attention, as famous Poles such as the writer and Nobel-Prize winner Henryk Sienkiewicz and the pianist Ignacy Paderewski raised awareness of the plight of the Polish people.

The road to independence

In November 1918, after 123 years of being controlled by other countries, Poland was finally granted its independence. Piłsudski was made head of state and the long process of rebuilding began: large parts of the country – and much of its beautiful architecture – had been destroyed.

Poland did not enjoy its hard-won freedom for long. In September 1939 Germany invaded Poland, and the Second World War began. Poland was partitioned once again – this time Germany and Russia divided it between them. Despite the collapse of their armies, many Poles fled the country and joined the armies opposing Germany. At the end of the Second World War, the leaders of the allied countries held a series of conferences to decide how to control the nations they had fought and what to do with the countries that had been occupied. The three great powers – the Soviet Union, the United States of America and Great Britain – established new borders for Poland and gave the country over to the influence of communist Soviet Russia.

When the borders changed, millions of Poles moved from the eastern territories to the west. It was nearly half a century before the Soviet influence in Poland declined. Several factors played a part in this – two of the most important were the social movement known as Solidarity and the influence of the Polish Pope John Paul II (see page 47). A new constitution was introduced in 1997 and since then Poland has improved international relations by joining many organisations, culminating in its membership of the European Union in 2004.

The country

Poland's landscape is divided into three main types –
the lowlands, the uplands and the mountainous regions.
Ancient rivers and lakes can be found all over the
countryside, and about 50 per cent of the land is arable.

The weather in Poland can be changeable, but
generally speaking, the climate is pleasant. In the
capital, Warsaw, the average temperature in the
hottest month (July) is 19°C and in the coldest
month (January) it can drop to -3°C. Across much
of the country rainfall is quite low, which means that
often there is not enough water to cultivate crops
efficiently. This is a particular problem in parts of
central Poland. In the mountainous regions in the
south of the country, however, there is a lot of water –
more than enough for the people living there.

Landscape

Much of the northern and central part of Poland
consists of flat plains, or lowlands. Thousands of
years ago, this area was covered by a massive ice sheet,
which moved southwards and back again as the
climate changed. It left behind hundreds of deposits
containing clay, sand and gravel, and 'erratic' boulders
scattered across the landscape. Some of these deposits
were left in small hills and ridges called moraines.
The movement of the ice sheet also created pits in the
ground, which grew to become broad river beds.

▲ All across the north of Poland, bordered by the
Baltic Sea, there are sandy beaches. Although it rarely
gets extremely hot in Poland, the summer climate is
perfect for sunbathing.

Rivers

Today, tributaries of the Oder and Vistula
rivers still flow westwards through these
ancient river beds. These are the two largest
rivers in Poland, and they both flow into the
Baltic Sea.

The Vistula flows freely through a series of
dams across the middle of the country, and its
banks have only been strengthened where it
flows through towns. It can be navigated down
the middle and downstream. The Oder, on
the other hand, is controlled through most
of its course, which means it can be used for
transporting goods between cities and towns.

◄ In the lowland areas left after the retreat of the
ice sheet, wind-blown sand has created these large
coastal dunes.

Although the water level in Polish rivers can change, it is usually quite low. Floods normally only occur in springtime, when the snow thaws, and at the beginning of summer, when there is more rainfall than at any other time of year.

In 1997, higher-than-usual levels of rainfall caused a major flood in the Oder Basin. It was so severe that it became known as 'the flood of the century'. Over 1,000 towns and villages were flooded; 3,000 km of roads, 2,000 km of railway lines and 944 bridges were completely destroyed. The Oder is controlled, which means that in some places it is very narrow and flows through a series of locks. During the flood, these could not contain the sudden surge of water. Around the Vistula River floodwaters poured over meadows in between the dams, but because these areas are largely uninhabited the damage was less severe.

The lowlands

There are three different regions that make up the Polish lowlands. The northern part is the Baltic coastline. This stretches for 500 km and has broad sandy beaches. In many places along the coastline, the wind has formed dunes – hills of sand. In other places, sea currents have carried the sand and built it up into long ridges with banks that are known as spits. In a few areas the sea has eroded the land, forming cliffs. This erosion has been a gradual process for many centuries and is still occurring today. A good example of erosion is the remains of the church walls in the village of Trzęsacz, which stand right on the cliff edge. Two hundred years ago the church was located 2 km from the coast!

▲ In 1997, the Vistula River flooded, causing extensive damage to many towns and cities. Here the waters flood the streets of Krakow.

▼ The Vistula River is the longest river in Poland (1,074 km); it flows through the middle of the country.

The spits cut off the gulfs from the sea and they become coastal lakes. Over the years, the sea fish that once lived in them have slowly adapted to the fresh water. The biggest coastal lake in Poland is Łebsko. On the Łebska Spit, which cuts the lake off from the sea, there are dunes that stretch to over 40 metres in height – the highest in the Baltic region. The wind is actually moving these dunes eastwards at a rate of 5 cm per year. The dunes are moving over an area that was once a forest; as the sand covered the trees, they were deprived of air and slowly died. You can still see the remains of old trees sticking out of the surface of the sand. In ancient times a Slavic tribe – the Słowiński people – inhabited this area. Some remnants of their lifestyle, including agricultural tools, have been found. The Słowiński National Park, which covers some of this region, takes its name from the tribe. The park attracts around 800,000 visitors a year, who go to see the impressive sand dunes and coastal lakes, as well as the diversity of flora and fauna that flourish there.

▲ *The fishing port of Łeba lies in the eastern part of the Łebska Spit and is a popular tourist destination.*

▼ *Behind the broad sand banks and high dunes of the coastline, lagoons and lakes have formed. This lagoon is situated near the town of Elbląg in the north of Poland.*

Along the eastern part of the coast there is a flat plains region – the delta of the Vistula River – called Żuławy Wiślane. This was shaped by the tributaries and canals around the Vistula. The landscape there is rather like the flat landscapes in the Netherlands, and this may be why it attracted Dutch settlers, who moved to Poland in the nineteenth century. They brought with them new farming techniques, including drainage systems, that improved the agricultural prospects of the region.

The Lake District

In the north-east of Poland lies the Lake District, which has the most diverse landscape. Here there are moraines, post-glacial lakes and rich forests. The soil here is very

◀ *The Mazurian Lakes form the eastern part of the Polish Lake District. The lakes are joined by a series of river channels and canals, and people come here to enjoy water-sports such as sailing, and to admire the views.*

sandy, though, and is not useful for agriculture. The lakes – of various shapes and sizes – lie in the small valleys created by hills, which reach an average height of 150 metres. The Lake District is divided by the Vistula River into two regions. The western part is called the Pomeranian Lake District and the eastern part is known as the Mazurian Lake District. Both are popular tourist areas, not only because of the beauty of the landscapes, but also because of the lively ethnic culture of the local people. The district of the Great Mazurian Lakes is particularly popular because of its clean environment. It has been nicknamed the 'green lungs of Poland', and is a paradise for fans of sailing and fishing.

Uplands and mountains

As you travel southwards in Poland, the landscape becomes more mountainous. The area known as the uplands is really the foothills of the mountains that lie in the far south of the country. The landscape is varied across this region – in Upper Silesia, for example, it is mainly industrial, while the Lublin Uplands are largely agricultural.

The mountain ranges in southern Poland include the Carpathian Mountains bordering the Czech Republic and the Sudeten Mountains on the border with Slovakia, as well as the Tatra and the Świętokrzyskie Mountains. They sit around 500 metres above sea level. From the highest mountain

in the Tatra range, all the different features of the landscape can be seen – sharp ridges, high snowy peaks, rivers, and deep valleys formed by the ancient glaciers. Both the uplands and the mountain regions of Poland are popular with walkers and climbers, for their peace and quiet, and their breathtaking views.

▶ *The Carpathian Mountains lie in the south of Poland, on the border with the Czech Republic. The highest peak is Gerlach (2,663 metres).*

Towns and cities

Warsaw is the capital of Poland and of the largest province, Mazovia. It is also the biggest city in Poland, with around 1.6 million inhabitants. Warsaw is home to all the most important church and state buildings, including religious centres, government offices and foreign embassies.

▲ *Today, Warsaw is developing rapidly. Modern skyscrapers are being built in the centre, and shopping malls are appearing on the outskirts of the city.*

▼ *The statue in the middle of Castle Square in Warsaw is the oldest monument in the city. It was erected in 1644 and commemorates King Sigismund Vasa III.*

Warsaw

Warsaw is one of Poland's greatest cultural centres and has been the focal point for some of the country's most dramatic events. Several times in the past, patriotic inhabitants of Warsaw fought against invaders. The city was severely damaged during German occupation in the Second World War – 20 per cent of the population was killed and 60 per cent of the buildings were destroyed. Many of these have now been carefully repaired or rebuilt, and Warsaw is a fascinating and thriving city once more. Several older monuments miraculously survived the war. Among these is the Wilanów Palace, built for King Jan Sobieski III in the seventeenth century. The Royal Castle (below) was not so lucky, and was razed to the ground in the war. It was rebuilt in magnificent style in the 1970s, and marks the beginning of the famous Royal Route between Castle Square and the two palaces of Wilanów and Lazienki.

▲ *This hoisting crane is one of the monuments of old Gdańsk that survived the war.*

▼ *Situated in the very north of Poland, on the Baltic Sea, Gdańsk is a thriving port.*

Gdańsk

Gdańsk lies in the very north of Poland. It is believed to have been founded in AD 997 by Prince Mieszko I. The earliest inhabitants of the area were Eastern Europeans, who travelled across the Baltic Sea in search of amber, a kind of gemstone. The succeeding generations of Poles, Dutch and Germans all contributed to the unique beauty of the town. As with many other Polish cities, Gdańsk was seriously damaged during the Second World War, and many of the current structures are the result of rebuilding in the second half of the twentieth century. However, some mementoes of the old town exist, including the Mariacki Church and several beautiful houses.

Gdańsk is mainly an industrial town. The biggest enterprises are the oil refinery and the shipyard, where the famous Solidarity movement was born (see page 46). A monument stands at the gate of the shipyard to commemorate the event.

This young boy is a street musician. He and his brother play music in the market square. 'I have been playing the violin since I was six,' he explains when he stops for a break. 'I am 14 now and still go to school. When classes are over, my brother and I go to our regular spot to play. Although most people know us, they don't give us any money. For that we depend on tourists, who can be very generous.' There are many buskers making money from tourists in towns and cities across Poland.

Elbląg

Elbląg, in the eastern part of the Polish lowlands, is an old seaport – connected with the Mazurian Lake District by the Elbląski River. The town was founded in 1237 by the Teutonic Knights, although at this time it was part of Prussia, not the Polish state. As well as many historical sites (several of which have been restored since the war), Elbląg is famous for its parks and gardens. There is also a lot to see in the surrounding area, including a Teutonic castle at Malbork. The town hosts a music festival in the summer, which is very popular with locals and tourists alike.

▲ Elbląg is a popular tourist destination; this town plan shows the key sites for visitors.

▶ Trams like this one in Elbląg are a common sight in the towns and cities of Poland.

Poznań

Poznań lies in the centre of Greater Poland (*Wielkopolska*). This was once the heart of the Polish state, and it was here that the ruler of Poland, Mieszko I, converted to Christianity over 1,000 years ago. The cathedral built on that site is one of the most important monuments in the city. Poznań is host to the International Trade Fair, which began in 1922 and has become one of the most prestigious events of its kind.

Gniezno

Gniezno is one of the oldest towns in Poland. Like Poznań, its history stretches right back to the birth of the Polish state. In the year AD 1000, the German emperor Otto III met the Polish ruler Boleslaus the Brave. The meeting is now known as the Summit of Gniezno. During the summit, the two rulers agreed to establish the first Polish archbishopric in Gniezno, and Boleslaus the Brave was awarded the right to be crowned as the first king of Poland. As a result, Gniezno became Poland's first capital and Polish kings were crowned here for more than 300 years.

There are many historical sites in Gniezno, including the great cathedral, which dates from the fourteenth century. In the cathedral lies the tomb of St Adalbertus, a bishop who was murdered while trying to convert to Christianity a Prussian tribe living in the Mazurian Lake District. In more recent times Gniezno has become a symbol of the reconciliation between Poland and Germany after the Second World War. Every few years summits are held at Gniezno, which are attended by key church officials and politicians from both countries.

62 per cent of the population of Poland lives in cities. However, there are many small towns with a population of less than 5,000. A city with more than 200,000 inhabitants is considered big. Warsaw, the capital city, has a population of over one and a half million.

▼ *The old market square in Poznań has been a meeting place for traders from both east and west for over 1,000 years.*

◀ The Branicki Palace in Białystok lies in the centre of the city and is the Branicki family residence. The palace has been nicknamed 'The Versailles of the North'.

Białystok

Białystok is situated in north-eastern Poland, and is the capital of the province of the same name. One of the most striking features of the city is the mixture of traditions from Eastern and Western Europe, and its ethnic and religious diversity. This is reflected most notably in its church buildings: there are Roman Catholic, Greek Catholic and Orthodox churches. In the surrounding area there are also villages populated by Islamic Tartars.

Katowice

Katowice, in southern Poland, is a typical industrial town. It began to grow and prosper in the middle of the nineteenth century, with the building of the Berlin railway that ran from Germany through Poland. It is a thriving modern town, and among the housing estates its industrial nature is very much in evidence – in the mine-hoist towers and factory chimneys. The town is also a renowned cultural and scientific centre, and is home to the University of Silesia and the Provincial Park of Culture and Recreation.

Łódź

Łódź is another relatively new city, but it is now the second largest in the country. Situated right in the middle of Poland, it was founded 200 years ago, when its textile industry began to develop, and it soon became a centre of international trade. The main street has many decorated houses, built in the ornamental style that was typical of the second half of the nineteenth century. Łódź is also home to Poland's film school and one of the country's finest museums of modern art. On the outskirts of the city is the medieval village of Piotrków Trybunalski.

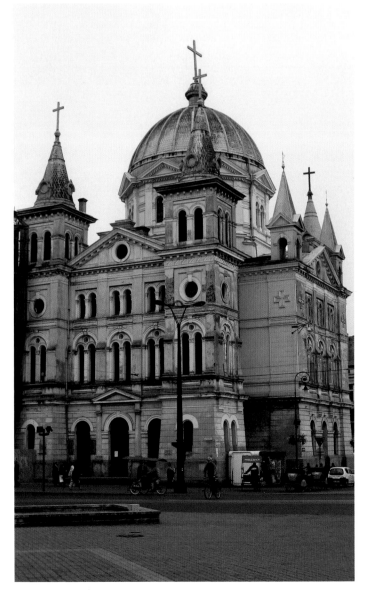

▶ Łódź is best known for its industrial architecture, such as the cotton mills, but it also has several other fine structures, like this baroque church.

Częstochowa

Częstochowa is regarded as the spiritual capital of Poland, and every year thousands of Catholics make a pilgrimage to the monastery of Jasna Góra ('Bright Mountain'). During the 'Swedish Flood', when invaders overpowered most of Poland, only Jasna Góra remained untaken, thanks to its location on a hill near the city, and the determination of the monks who defended it. The famous painting *The Lady of Częstochowa* (also known as the 'Black Madonna') is housed here and is worshipped by Catholic pilgrims not only from Poland, but also from neighbouring countries, who come on foot to Częstochowa during the major religious festival in August.

Wrocław

Situated on the Oder River in south-west Poland, Wrocław is a city full of parkland and historic architecture. The biggest zoo in Poland can be found here.

▲ *Pilgrims flock to the church of Jasna Góra, high on the hill above Częstochowa.*

▼ *The main square in Wrocław is characteristic of the fine architecture to be found all over this ancient city, situated at the foot of the Sudeten Mountains.*

▲ The citizens of Krakow wanted to build a church to rival the royal cathedral on Wawel Hill, so they constructed this – the Church of Our Lady.

▲ Wawel Cathedral has no fewer than 18 chapels, and is the final resting place of many Polish kings.

Krakow

Krakow is one of the most beautiful cities in Poland, and for centuries it served as the country's capital. The most famous building in Krakow is the Royal Castle, on Wawel Hill. The site itself is ancient – people lived here more than 3,000 years ago. The present castle was built in the sixteenth century for King Sigismund I, although Polish kings lived here for more than 500 years before this. The centre of Krakow was once surrounded by fortified walls, and parts of the crumbling remains can still be seen. The best-preserved sections of the ancient fortress are the Barbakan stronghold and the Floriańska Gate.

Wieliczka

Wieliczka lies in southern Poland. The town is famous for its salt mine, which has been in use for more than 700 years. In the eighteenth century, a visitor to the mines commented that it was as magnificent as the Egyptian pyramids! Salt used to be a valuable trading product and Wieliczka was the heart of a thriving industry.

◀ Despite the persecution of Polish Jews during the Second World War, many of Krakow's synagogues survived.

The mine is a complex system of underground galleries, stretching for over 200 km, which connect around 2,000 'rooms' or caverns across nine different levels. Over the centuries, mine-workers developed a tradition of carving statues in the salt. The result of this centuries-old custom is a subterranean city made up of churches, altars, reliefs and statues. There is an underground museum, and a health spa has even been built in the mine; people visit this, believing that the air in the mine, saturated with salt, has a healing effect – particularly for those suffering from illnesses like bronchitis.

The unique nature and historic and artistic value of the Wieliczka salt mine have resulted in it becoming part of UNESCO's World Heritage list. Every year, around one million visitors go to marvel at the sight.

▲ *The salt mine in Wieliczka is a maze of huge caverns with statues and friezes all carved out of the salt.*

Zakopane

Zakopane's mountain scenery once attracted writers and artists, but today it is more popular as a base for hikers and skiers. Despite being a great tourist spot, the town is famous for maintaining many regional traditions. Visitors to Zakopane can hear ethnic music and dialects – and try a number of traditional dishes.

▼ *The town of Zakopane lies in the foothills of the Tatra mountain range.*

People and culture

Poland has a population of nearly 40 million. More than 97 per cent of these people are native Poles; the remaining three per cent is made up of other ethnic groups. In Europe, only Greece and Portugal have smaller minority populations.

Poland's minorities include Germans (around 153,000), Belarusians (50,000), Ukrainians (31,000), and gypsies or Roma (13,000). However, among the Polish nationals there are several different ethnic groups that each have their own traditions. These groups include the Silesians, Kashubs and Górale

'My friend is getting married. In Poland, it is traditional for guests to take flowers to the ceremony and present them to the couple. After the service there will be a reception where we will have a meal and dance to lively polka music.'

▼ It is traditional to pin money to the bride's dress at a wedding. Here, a bride and groom collect coins that have been tossed outside the church for good luck.

(mountaineers). As well as varying customs, these groups can be distinguished by slight differences in language. On special occasions, Polish people wear colourful national costumes. The most spectacular are those worn by people from the Krakow and Łowicz regions, and by the mountaineers.

A mature society

Poland is considered to be a 'mature' society. This means that it has a high percentage of older people. Although there are more children (up to the age of 15) than people over 65, the percentage of young people is decreasing every year, while the number of old people is increasing as people live longer. The average life expectancy for women there is 78 and for men, 70. Poland has quite a low birth-rate – more people are dying than are being born. Poland also has a migration deficit – that is, more people emigrate abroad than migrate to the country.

▲ Folk musicians in national dress playing in the market square in Poznań.

Poles abroad

Twelve million Polish people live in other countries. The majority of them – around eight million – have emigrated to the USA. Cities such as Chicago, Detroit and New York have high Polish populations. Germany has more Polish people than any other European country – around 1.5 million Poles live there.

Although the rate of unemployment in Poland is high – around 20 per cent – the quality of life in the country is not poor. The number of Poles owning cars and other technologies such as computers has increased dramatically in the past few years. Fifteen million people in Poland now own mobile phones. Poles also enjoy better health than people in many other European countries.

◀ The average age of the Polish population is increasing, as people are living longer, but the birth-rate is declining.

Religion in Poland

The majority of Polish people (around 95 per cent) are Roman Catholics, and the Church plays an important part in the spiritual lives of many Poles. More than 75 per cent attend church services regularly. During the Partitions of the eighteenth century (see page 7), the Church helped the people to preserve a sense of national identity and played a significant role in regaining independence. It also provided spiritual support for many Poles during the communist regime after the Second World War.

There are a number of other Churches in Poland, including the Greek and Russian Orthodox, and Protestant offshots – the largest of which is the Lutheran-Augsburg Church.

(see page 7)

St Andrew's Night

One of Poland's most popular holidays is St Andrew's Night, or *Andrzejki*, which is celebrated on 30 November. Traditionally, on this day young Polish people tell one another's fortunes. To do this, they switch off the lights and light a candle. Holding the candle over a bowl of cold water, they let some hot wax drip on to the water, where it hardens and forms a shape that floats on the surface. The fortune teller then 'reads' or interprets the shape to reveal what the coming year will bring. The custom began many years ago, when it was intended to predict the future of unmarried girls – particularly their propects for a good marriage.

National symbols

Poland's national colours are white and red; the choice of these colours dates back to the pennants used by medieval kings. They are represented in the national flag as two equally sized horizontal bands. The top half is white and the bottom red. The national emblem depicts a white eagle (the symbol of the Piast dynasty) with a gold crown, and this appears on the red background. The national anthem – Dabrowski's *Mazurek* – expresses love for the country and faith in the strength of its people.

Government

Poland is a democratic state. The parliament consists of two chambers (called *Sejm* and *Senat*), and members are elected to these every four years. They are the highest levels of legislative authority. Executive power is exercised by the government and the president. The president is the head of state and the supreme commander of the armed forces. General elections are held in Poland every five years.

▲ *A nun speaks to a young girl in the street. Religion plays a large part in most people's lives.*

◄ *The currency in Poland is złoty; this is a 100-złoty note, which is the equivalent of around 17 British pounds or 24 euros.*

◄ The Presidential Palace in Warsaw has been the residence of Poland's president since 1994.

The country is divided into 16 provinces. Each province is run by a governor – appointed by the government – and a provincial assembly, elected by the citizens. The provinces are made up of districts, which are subdivided into communes. Districts and communes are units of self-government.

Today, Poland maintains good relationships with all its neighbouring countries and is very active in the international arena. It was one of the founding members of the United Nations and its army participates in many peace missions – including Kosovo, Afghanistan and Iraq. Poland is a member of NATO and, since 1 May 2004, of the European Union.

Famous Poles

One of the best-known Poles is Nicolas Copernicus (1473–1543), who was the first person to suggest that the Earth moved around the Sun, instead of the other way round as most people believed at that time. Other famous Polish scientists include Marie Curie (1867–1934), who discovered the chemical elements radium and polonium. Pianist and composer Fryderyk Chopin (1810–49) is also a well-loved Polish man. The most famous Pole of the twentieth century was was the last pope, John Paul II (see page 47).

▼ A statue of Nicolaus Copernicus (left), a portrait of Fryderyk Chopin (middle) and a photograph of Marie Curie (right).

Education

Poland has a good education system, and Polish children receive the same standard of education as those in Western Europe. The system is the same across the whole country and there are five levels of education.

The first stage is kindergarten, for children aged three to five. After kindergarten children move on to primary school until the age of 13. They do not take any exams at the end of this stage. They then move on to lower secondary school until they are 16. Primary school and lower secondary are compulsory in Poland – all children must attend school between the ages of five and 16. At the end of lower secondary school pupils take exams to go on to further education. This falls into two categories: general secondary schools and vocational secondary schools. These are for children aged 17 to 19 or 20. If students want to continue studying after this they go to universities.

▼ *Nicola attends this primary school in Gdańsk. She will leave when she is 13 and move on to a lower secondary school.*

◀ *Children play outside a village school.*

School years last almost 10 months and are divided into two semesters. The school year begins on 1 September and ends in the middle of June. The summer holidays last throughout July and August, and pupils have other breaks at Christmas, New Year and Easter. There is another short break in January or February. The school week begins on Monday and ends on Friday or Saturday, depending on the local authorities.

Exams

Polish children take their first exams at the end of lower secondary school. Depending on their exam results, they can choose to attend a general or vocational secondary school. Vocational schools focus on practical subjects, while general secondaries are more academic. Although this stage is not compulsory, most Polish children continue their education. The exams students take at the end of upper secondary level can gain them admission to university.

At the moment many young people in Poland take their education as far as they can, because they realise that a better education will improve their job prospects.

▶ *The University of Warsaw was established in 1816.*

Although there is an education curriculum in Poland, it is quite flexible. The Ministry of Education sets up the minimum requirements at each stage, and this forms the basis for the syllabus. However, the teachers can adapt the syllabus to suit the conditions of the school and the needs and abilities of the students. This is also true of the text books that are used in schools, although the Ministry of Education has to approve them. There are no fees for attending a public school, but pupils have to buy their own text books and take them to school every day.

▼ This lesson plan shows some typical weekly lessons for a pupil in a lower secondary school (between the ages of 13 and 16). The optional classes at the end of the day might be extra foreign language lessons or sports.

The number of lessons in a week depends on the age of the pupils. In primary schools there are usually 23 lessons per week, with 28 in lower secondary schools and 31 in general and vocational secondary schools. The curriculum includes several core subjects, such as maths, the three sciences and Polish language. Many schools also place importance on technological subjects such as IT.

Typical lesson plan for a lower secondary school

	Monday	Tuesday	Wednesday	Thursday	Friday
1	maths	chemistry	English	art	Polish
2	biology	maths	physics	geography	Polish
3	Polish	English/PE (in groups)	religion	English/PE (in groups)	physics
4	English/PE (in groups)	Polish	maths	Polish	English/PE (in groups)
5	geography	history	maths		lesson with class teacher
6	history	technology	PE		biology
7					civic education
8	optional classes				

▶ *A girl browses in her school library.*

Another important subject is foreign languages, and students are required to study at least one language throughout their education. Teaching of foreign languages begins in the fourth year of primary school. The most common languages learnt in Polish schools are English, German, Russian and French. Some schools also offer lessons in Spanish or Italian. Religious Studies (Roman Catholicism) is taught as an optional subject in schools. Students also have three lessons of physical education per week.

It is possible to specialise in particular areas by taking classes that are grouped as 'paths'. These are made up of similar subjects. Humanities includes Polish, foreign languages, history and social studies. The Mathematical and Natural Science path consists of maths, biology, geography, physics and chemistry. There are also paths that cover issues such as environmental education, art, European education and intercultural education. These are very popular among students in Polish schools, as is computer studies.

The school day
School starts at eight o'clock and each lesson lasts 45 minutes. The number of students in each class depends on where the school is. In busy towns and cities there can be up to 40 pupils per class, but there may be only half that number in schools in rural areas. Across the whole country there is an average of 21 students in each class.

After the normal lessons of the day, pupils can take part in optional classes, such as sports. Learning foreign languages (particularly English) in additional classes is becoming increasingly common. Learning how to use the Internet is also popular, as it is not only educational but also provides entertainment and helps to develop students' personal interests.

◀ *A small primary school in Rybnik, in southern Poland.*

▲ *These pupils are studying at a famous forestry school in Bialowieza – a vocational secondary school.*

Many Polish children live in small villages in the countryside, where there are no schools, so they often have to commute to the nearest town. They take special buses, which are free of charge, called *gimbuses*. The name comes from the words *gimnazjum* (the Polish name for lower secondary school) and autobus. They are painted bright orange so they can be seen from a distance. The journey to school can be time-consuming, though. Children in villages often help their parents on their farms, so their school day can be long and tiring.

School uniforms are not obligatory in Poland and only a few schools have them. Usually, pupils are allowed to wear their own clothes and express themselves freely.

'We go to school in Braniewo,' Amanda tells us.

'There are no schools in our village, so every day we take the school bus to town and back,' her friend Elisabeth adds.

'We get up early every morning, because the bus arrives at 7 o'clock,' Amanda explains.

'We have had a lovely two months' holiday, but school starts again next week,' Elisabeth says. However, the girls don't mind going back to school – they can get bored during the long summer holidays.

Cuisine

One of the best ways to understand a country and its culture is to learn about its food and the favourite dishes its people cook. In Poland, some of the most delicious meals are the traditional dishes from different regions.

Polish cuisine is quite heavily influenced by other cultures and today you can taste dishes from all over the world in Poland. Foreign delicacies were first introduced in the houses of the nobility, as people travelled further and brought back new ideas to Poland. Gradually the influences of Italian, French, Russian, Hungarian and Jewish cooking began to show in the Polish kitchen.

What we would call modern Polish cuisine became popular in the nineteenth century, and traditional dishes are now passed down from generation to generation. Eating habits and recipes are strongly connected with the climate, culture and religion of a region.

▼ *This cheese stand is advertising a Polish speciality — oscypek — cheese made from sheep's milk.*

Krakow sausage is probably the best-known sausage in Poland. According to the Polish recipe it is made of 80 per cent pork, 10 per cent beef and 10 per cent fat. It is seasoned with pepper, fresh garlic and cumin. The sausage is smoked in hot smoke until it is golden brown, and then braised or cooked. After it has been left to cool down, it is smoked again, in warm smoke, to give it a dark-brown colour.

Traditional Polish foods include a variety of soups (hot and cold), sauerkraut (pickled cabbage), pickled cucumber, potatoes, pork and dairy products such as cheese.

Popular dishes are *bigos* (sliced sausage, pork and beef stewed in sauerkraut), *pierogi* (dumplings), goat's cheese, mushrooms, tripe, sirloin and different sausages.

▲ Żurek is a sour soup made with egg and sausage.

Poland has applied for EU certificates that will allow the country to produce certain regional products according to original recipes and sell them across Europe. Such products include *oscypek*, plum vodka from Nowy Sącz, some kinds of dried or smoked sausages, mushroom dishes, fruit and vegetable preserves, soups such as barszcz, dishes made of potatoes, and various kinds of *pierogi*.

Christmas

Christmas and Easter are very important in Poland. They are not only celebrated as religious festivals, when families get together, but they are also the times when many customs are observed, including the cooking of traditional dishes.

Christmas Eve is the most important evening of the year. It starts when the first star appears in the sky. All members of the family sit at the table and share special wafers. This custom, unique to Poland, is based on the ancient tradition of families sharing bread, and is an important Polish tradition. The table is set with a tablecloth and candles so the meal looks festive. Many people still put a handful of hay under the tablecloth to remind them of the stable in Bethlehem. An extra place is always set for an unexpected guest.

Recipe for barszcz

Ingredients
12 medium-sized beetroots
1 onion, chopped
1/4 cup of water
The juice of 1 lemon
1 teaspoon of sugar
1 cup of vegetable broth
Salt and pepper
1/2 cup of sour cream

Wash the beetroots; peel them and cook them with the onion in the water until they are soft. Add the lemon juice, sugar, salt and pepper. Let the mixture stand overnight. Blend it and add the broth. Heat the mixture and add the sour cream before serving.

Traditional dishes eaten on Chrismas Eve include mushroom soup with noodles, fish soup with cream and noodles or beetroot soup with small dumplings stuffed with mushrooms. Fish is also popular, and different types are eaten at this time of year – carp or herring cooked in jelly, fried or served with a sauce. The traditional cabbage and dumplings or noodles are also served, with mushrooms or poppy seeds. For dessert the Poles eat a compote of dried fruit such as cranberries, poppy seeds with honey or poppy-seed pie, gingerbread or biscuits.

▲ *Christmas is an important holiday in Poland, and people put festive decorations on the table.*

Easter

Easter, the most important holiday in the Christian tradition, begins with the blessing of the food. A great deal of effort goes into preparing Easter breakfast, which consists of several cold dishes. On Holy Saturday, the day before Easter, the Poles carry baskets to church so they can be blessed. The baskets contain samples of everything they will have for breakfast: a leg of lamb decorated with a red flag, twigs and flowers, eggs, sausage, slices of ham, pastry, salt, pepper and horseradish. All these items have a symbolic meaning. The lamb with the flag symbolises Christ, while the twigs, flowers and eggs stand for the new life that Christ gives through His Resurrection. The tradition of blessing the Easter breakfast began in the twelfth century, and until the eighteenth century priests would actually visit people's homes to bless the meal. Since then, though, it has become more practical to take a basket to church.

One of the most traditional Easter foods is hardboiled eggs. These are often painted, or patterns are scratched on the shell. Patterns vary depending on the region. The customary meat to eat at Easter is pork, in different forms. Smoked or boiled ham, white sausages (boiled or roasted) served with grated horseradish and vinegar or lemon juice, are particularly popular. The Poles also have a traditional Easter cake called *mazurek*, made of cream, nuts, raisins and dried fruit on a wafer base.

Eating out

Eating out has become popular in Poland in the past few years. Under the communist regime, eating at restaurants was not encouraged. Today, however, Poland has a fast-food culture like many other nations. American and Asian dishes are served in numerous fast-food restaurants. Traditional European cuisine, especially Italian and French, is also becoming popular. A recent trend, which has benefited locals and the tourist trade, has been the opening of new restaurants that specialise in typical Polish food. A traditional saying in Poland is 'a hungry Pole is an angry Pole'.

◀ *A breaded pork chop with sauerkraut and potatoes.*

Transport

Poland lies right in the heart of Europe. This means that the shortest routes from Eastern to Western Europe, and from north to south, cut right through Poland. The fact that much of the country is made up of flat lowlands has helped with the building of roads and railways.

▼ Signs indicating main roads are green with white writing. The route numbers are white in a red rectangle.

Two of the most important road routes are the A2, which runs from Germany to the Russian capital Moscow, and the A4, which runs from Germany to Lvov and Kiev in the Ukraine. Two new roads are being built with the help of funding from the European Union. These will run from Estonia, Latvia and Lithuania to Warsaw, and from Gdańsk to the southern border and as far as the Adriatic Sea.

▼ People use buses or trams to travel around locally.

◀ A small train, typical of those that run on local lines.

Most people in Poland travel by car. The number of people owning cars has increased dramatically in recent years, and by 2002 there were 300 cars per 1,000 inhabitants – close to the European average. There are more than 365,000 km of roads across Poland, but only 400 km of these are motorways.

▲ An intercity train stops at Swarzedz station. These high-speed trains are being introduced across Poland.

Railways

Poland has one of the highest numbers of railway tracks in Europe, but in recent years the transportation of people and goods by rail has declined as more people travel by road. As in most European countries, it is really only the busy main railway lines that are profitable, and the smaller lines are slowly closing down. At the same time, railway tracks that can accommodate new high-speed trains are being built or modernised. These will run from Warsaw to other key Polish cities, including Krakow, Katowice, Wrocław, Poznań, Szczecin and Gdańsk. These intercity trains can reach speeds of 160 kph and are cheaper and quicker than travelling by car. In many cases they are even better than travelling by plane. Equally fast Euro City trains link Warsaw to Berlin, Moscow, Prague and Bratislava.

Shipping

Polish shipping has recently undergone significant changes, and the former state merchant marine fleet has been privatised. Economic zones were established and this meant that the Polish deep-sea fishing fleet could

▲ *From Gdańsk it is possible to take a ferry to Nynäshamn, just south of Stockholm in Sweden.*

no longer fish anywhere it liked, and it has had to be closed down. Today, only a few fishing boats patrol the small 'Polish' fishing zone in the Baltic.

Transport by sea is well established in Poland. There are three main ports on the Baltic coast in the north – Gdańsk, Gdynia and Szczecin-Świnoujście. Ferries owned by Polish companies, as well as those from other European countries, sail regularly from Świnoujście and Gdynia to Sweden and Denmark. However, the ports used to serve many more ships than they do now. The decrease in traffic in Poland's ports is largely due to the drop in the importance of coal in foreign trade. Coal used to be Poland's most important and lucrative export, and was mass produced and shipped to countries all over Europe, but today there is far less demand for coal.

Poland also uses its inland water courses for transporting goods between cities. The inland shipping routes actually stretch to around 4,000 km, but the majority of them are quite shallow and can only be used by small boats. The exception to this is the Oder River, which has been regulated and joined with Upper Silesia by the Gliwicki Canal. Even here, though, shipping has to cease during hot dry summers; the last time this happened was in 2003.

▼ *LOT is Poland's national airline company.*

Aviation

LOT is Poland's national airline. It has a fleet of 50 long-distance aircraft, connecting Poland with 27 other countries. There are three international airports in Poland – in Warsaw, Krakow and Gdańsk. The Fryderyk Chopin airport in Warsaw is particularly convenient, as it is located only 6 km from the city centre. The most popular destinations from Poland are the USA and Canada. Domestic flights are less popular – for many inland journeys, travelling by train is just as fast and much cheaper.

The economy

The structure of the economy in Poland is similar to
that of other European countries – services (66 per cent),
industry (31 per cent) and agriculture (3 per cent). The
economy has stablilised over the past decade and since
joining the European Union Poland has received funding
that will help improve things further.

▼ *A farmer uses his bicycle
to herd his cattle down a
street in Bialowieza.*

Arable and dairy farming

Poland produces enough food to supply
its population and allow a surplus. The
country's climate, landscape and soil
combine to create good conditions for
growing crops and for breeding cattle and
other livestock. There is a lot of farmland
in Poland – the equivalent of nearly half
a hectare per person. However, the distri-
bution of farming is uneven – there are
too many small farms and too many people
employed in this sector. An average farm
in Poland is about eight hectares and
11 per cent of the population are farmers.

Many of the smaller farms find it hard
to make enough money, so some farmers
take on additional employment. Some
of them turn their farms into tourist
attractions. Here, people who live in cities

can go and see how country people
live and try regional dishes – and
children learn that milk comes from
cows not containers!

The majority of small farms use
traditional methods of growing crops
and breeding farm animals, and as a
result agricultural products are healthy
and free from artificial products. Many
farmers use only natural or ecologically
safe fertilisers and pesticides.

◀ *Cabbages are harvested and then
transported to auctions.*

Other than cattle for meat and milk, the main crops grown by farmers in Poland are wheat, rye, potatoes and sugar beets. Growing wheat requires very fertile soil, but rye and potatoes can be grown even in the northern and eastern areas, where the soil is poor. Barley and oats are also produced in small quantities in Poland, as well as hops, flax and hemp.

Another of Poland's main produce is fruit. Apple juice from Polish apples is exported to countries all over the world. Polish plums, strawberries, raspberries and blackcurrants are also well known in Europe.

Breeding sheep used to be common in Poland, but in recent years sheep farming has become less popular. Some farmers still keep small herds of sheep, but these are mainly in the mountains, where the sheepskins are used to make coats and the milk is used to produce the regional cheese *oscypek*.

The breeding of race horses is a long-standing tradition in Poland. Auctions of Arabian horses are held in Janów Podlaski and attract horse lovers and buyers from many different countries. Farmers all over Poland used to use horses to help plough the fields, but today draught horses – as they are known – are decreasing in numbers and are found mainly on farms in the mountainous regions in the south of the country.

▼ *Potatoes are one of the most important crops grown in Poland, and a major export.*

▲ *Polish farmers used to use horses to help in the fields, but in most areas today modern machinery is used.*

▶ *A copper-melting plant in Legnica, in eastern Poland.*

Industry

Polish industry started to develop during the period of Partitions in the eighteenth century, and has declined and been rebuilt several times since then. After the Second World War all the factories were nationalised and the process of industrialisation really began. Heavy industry – producing equipment for other industry sectors – developed rapidly, while light industry – making products for consumption – began to decline. However, it soon became obvious that neither type of industry was modern enough to compete with the

▼ *The Elbląg branch of the Alstom company, which builds transport such as ships and trains.*

goods produced by more developed countries. It was only in the 1990s that the process of modernisation began. Many enterprises were privatised and new technologies were introduced. The process of modernisation is still going on in Poland, and it is encompassing all sections of the country's economy.

Poland is a big producer of passenger cars. In addition, Polish manufacturers build spare parts for foreign car companies such as Fiat, Daewoo, Volkswagen and General Motors.

The industry sector that manufactures construction materials, especially cement, bricks, mineral-wool and various types of plastics, is developing rapidly in Poland. Polish furniture, clothes, medicines, cosmetics and food products are also highly valued in the world markets. The future for Poland's economy is looking bright, as Polish companies begin to move into the electronics and engineering industries, and to further develop the existing industries of construction and agriculture.

Energy

The power sector, producing energy and fuel, is well developed. Poland is an important producer of two different types of coal – black and brown. Both of these are used to create electricity; in Poland, only 2 per cent of electricity is produced by hydroelectric power plants.

▲ *This factory makes parts for passenger cars – often the cars themselves come from other European countries or the USA.*

None of the power plants in Poland uses oil or natural gas, because there are not many domestic sources and the country has to import them – mainly from Russia. As well as coal, Poland also has rich deposits of sulphur and copper ores that contain useful compounds. The sulphur is turned into sulphuric acid, which is used in several different industries. Copper is a valuable metal and once the copper ores have been mined the copper and many of its by-products can be very useful.

Import and export

Although the Polish economy is improving, Poland is still something of a developing country. Privatisation and modernisation of industry are steps forward, but it may be many years before the positive effects are felt. Changing industry in this way requires importing many goods from other countries, and often the import value is higher than the export value. For example, the value of imported machines and transport vehicles is twice as high as the export value of such goods. Crude oil and natural gas imported from Russia are the most expensive imports, whereas the export of coal is low, and getting lower.

Poland's most important trade partner is Germany. One third of Polish export value and one quarter of import value come from trading with Germany. This is the only country with which Poland has a trade surplus. With other trade partners – Italy, the Netherlands, France, the UK and Russia – Poland has a trade deficit. Because of this, it had to apply for credit from the World Bank for its development plans. The debts amount to £30 billion, but this is being cleared by a regular repayment scheme.

▶ *Poland has one of the largest ship-building industries in the world; this is a shipyard in Gdańsk.*

The environment

Over the last 10 years, the state of Poland's natural environment has improved considerably, and at the moment Poland's environmental problems are no worse than those of other countries in Europe. Although some damage was caused during the intensive industry development after 1945, measures are being taken to rectify this.

There are several reasons for this change. The most important is that environmental awareness has improved – people realised that damage to the environment can lead to disaster, the spread of disease, and even death.

Environmental conditions in Poland are diverse. Industrial zones in the big cities, and particularly in Upper Silesia, suffer from pollution. In the north-east of Poland, between the Vistula and Narew Rivers and the eastern border of the country, the natural environment is much cleaner. Only environmentally friendly sections of industry are developed there.

▲ Areas in the north-east of the country are so clean that they have been nicknamed 'the green lungs of Poland'.

◄ Air pollution spews out of the chimneys of a coal-powered plant at the Gdańsk shipyard.

Air

Until recently industry was the main cause of pollution. Thanks to the closure of unused factories, the introduction of new, environmentally friendly technologies and the installation of filters on factory fans, the situation has improved dramatically. Almost all energy in Poland is produced from coal. In the process of burning this coal, enormous amounts of pollution can be created. Power plants are equipped with modern filters and, as a result, over the last 10 years the emission of sulphur dioxide, nitrous oxide and dust has been considerably reduced. Today, the main cause of pollution is the car. The number of cars in Poland is increasing and they are not used economically – in cities only one third of cars carry more than one passenger. In many urban areas the pollution by exhaust fumes contributes 60 per cent of the total pollution.

▼ *Autumn colours in the Bieszcady National Park.*

The violet

A Polish legend tells the story of the violet. The tale is set in the kingdom of the Wends, a Slavic tribe living on the borders of the River Elbe. Long ago, an evil god called Czorneboh ruled the Wends. He brought them nothing but suffering. The only good thing about Czorneboh was his lovely daughter. When the Christian missionaries came to the kingdom of the Wends, Czorneboh did all he could to resist these preachers of the faith. But the Christians were stronger – they destroyed Czorneboh's evil power, and he was transformed into a rock. His beautiful daughter responded by turning herself into a violet that blossoms once every 100 years at the foot of her father the rock. Legend says that whoever succeeds in picking this violet on Walpurgis Night – the night from 30 April to 1 May – will receive Czorneboh's lovely daughter as his wife, with all his riches as her dowry.

Water

Water is also becoming cleaner. The level of rainfall is quite low in Poland compared to that of neighbouring countries, and the amount of water per person is one of the lowest in Europe. Water deficit is particularly acute in the lowland areas of central Poland. Agriculture suffers during dry summers. Periodical lack of water affects industry and some big cities, but there has never been a severe lack of drinking water.

▶ *Hay stacks in summer in the Tatra Mountains.*

Water is transported by pipes for great distances to Łódź, Katowice, Krakow and Warsaw. In these cities, it is purified using chlorine and ozone. This actually worsens its flavour, which is why in Warsaw and some other cities drinking water is often drawn from deep-water wells. In order to improve water quality many new sewage plants have been built, although they are not available in every town. Thanks to the newly built sewage plants, rivers are much cleaner than they were 10 years ago. Lakes and rivers are no longer polluted by fertilisers and pesticides used in agriculture, because farmers use them more carefully. The number of fish and other species living in rivers and lakes across Poland is increasing as the water becomes cleaner.

Recently efforts have been made to protect and preserve the natural environment. Certain areas have been established where plants, animals, water and the landscape as a whole are protected. There are several of these national parks and nature reserves throughout Poland. Particular objects such as old trees, unusual rocks, stones and caves are also designated as natural monuments.

▶ *The Suwalki Nature Reserve in eastern Poland.*

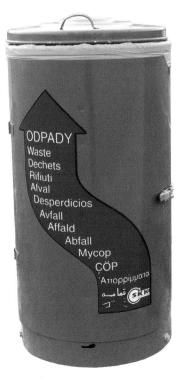

Enviromental education

The change in attitude towards environmental issues has been assisted by schools and the media. Even though school curricula do not include ecology as a separate subject, ecological issues are covered in geography, biology, physics, chemistry, and even Polish and history. Pupils not only study theoretical problems, but also participate in activities arranged for the benefit of the local environment. Sometimes these are campaigns such as collecting litter in forests on Earth Day, but they also include long-term activities that focus on developing ecological awareness for the future. With the help of their teachers, students are trying to accomplish an 'ecological alphabet' – a project that lists ways of protecting the environment. For example, by not choosing disposable products that pollute the environment (like drinks in glass bottles, plastic containers, products made of PVC), separating waste into items that can be recycled and those that can't, using cleaning products that do not contain phosphates, using public transport instead of private cars, and saving energy.

Nature and tourism

Poland might not be as popular as the Mediterranean as a holiday destination, but it has a lot to offer foreign visitors. More and more people travel to Poland every year to enjoy its customs, scenery and architecture.

▼ *Climbing is a popular sport in the mountains of southern Poland.*

Poland's rich landscape is its greatest tourist attraction. Large parts of the country used to be covered by forest, but today many of these have been cut down and the land is now used for farming. However, there have been moves recently to return the land to its natural state, and areas that have little agricultural value are being reforested. At the moment, more than a quarter of the country is woodland – mostly coniferous forests with pine and fir trees. Mixed forests with oak and beech trees can also be found in some parts of the country. The beaches, lakes and rivers are other attractive parts of the landscape.

The woods, fields and meadows give shelter to wild animals. Many of the species are endangered, so they are partially or completely under protection. Grey hares were common in Poland until quite recently, but now they are in danger of extinction and are protected during the breeding period. There is currently a campaign to ban the hunting of these animals.

On the other hand, the strictly protected aurochs have recently increased in number, so some of them are being culled. Beavers and moose are in a similar situation. The wolf population is also considered too large. In the eastern part of the country, wolves have killed large numbers of deer, and recently attacks on herds of livestock have been reported.

National parks

On the plains and hills of the Polish lowlands, where agriculture first developed, the remaining forests are now protected as national parks or landscape parks. This large area is divided into the Wielkopolska Lowlands, the Mazowiecko-Podlaska Lowlands and the Śląska Lowlands. Here, tourists can find the most untouched landscapes Poland has to offer: wide river valleys with natural meadows and flora, where large numbers of waterfowl build their nests. Birds are protected in the Biebrza, Narew and Ujście Wart National Parks, and in many nature reserves.

In the Carpathian Mountains there are two national parks. In the Tatra National Park various types of vegetation can be found depending how high above sea level it is. Up to 1,200 metres there are beech-fir woods, above them pine trees, then dwarf mountain pines and meadows. Fauna includes chamois, groundhogs, bears and eagles. In the Polish part of the Carpathians there are also the Pieniny

Aurochs

An auroch is a type of wild bison. The story of aurochs in Poland is extraordinary. In 1919 the last auroch living in the wild died in the Białowieska Forest, and the only examples of the species lived in zoos. From these, 12 aurochs suitable for breeding were selected and kept in an isolated breeding station. A few years later, in 1959, they were re-introduced to the Białowieska Forest. Five years later the first calf was born. Soon there were so many of them in the forest that they needed to be moved to other places – some were even shot. The Białowieska Forest is still their main habitat, but they can be also found in the Bieszczady Mountains, in the Borecka Forest (the Mazurian Lake District) and in the Pilskie Woods (the Pomeranian Lake District).

Mountains, where rafting trips are organised every summer on the Dunajec River, which is famous for its beautiful ravines. The Bieszczady Mountains are home to the Bieszczady National Park, where vast meadows and beech forests are the habitat of bears, wolves, lynxes, wildcats and even aurochs.

Forest-dominated national parks include the Kampinos and the Białowieska. In Kampinos, bordering the capital city of Warsaw, there are moose and lynxes, both of which are being reintroduced into their natural habitat. The Białowieska National Park features on UNESCO's World Heritage list. This is the last natural forest with aurochs – the biggest land mammals in Europe.

Tourist areas

The Baltic coast in Poland is famous for its vast beaches. It is a perfect place for swimming, walking and collecting amber, which used to be called the 'gold of the Baltic'. Amber is rinsed out from the sand by special machines and sold in jewellery shops. The most precious pieces of amber are those with insects preserved inside them, usually flies or mosquitoes.

Poland is not only an attractive tourist destination because of its scenery, though. People also visit the country to admire its architecture. Although parts of many cities were destroyed during the Second World War and have been rebuilt since then, thousands of old buildings survive. The architecture is

mainly Gothic and Baroque. Tourists also go to visit the churches and castles, and admire the wooden shrines that are scattered all over the countryside. There are several 'tourist trails', including those that take in the Cistercian monasteries and churches, and Teutonic castles. In the east and south of Poland there are many genuine examples of wooden architecture, especially small Catholic and Eastern Orthodox churches.

Polish religious and festive customs are both original and spectacular, and are well worth participating in. These include pilgrimages to the places of religious interest, Corpus Christi Day processions, food blessings at Easter, and nativity plays at Christmas.

▼ *Krakow's amazing old buildings attract thousands of tourists every year.*

Poland in the EU

After the Second World War, Europe was divided for more than 50 years. The independent trade-union movement known as Solidarity, led by Lech Walesa (see below), greatly contributed to the collapse of the post-war communist regime in Poland, and since 1989 it has been a democratic country.

In 1994 Poland signed the Association Agreement with the European Union and applied for EU membership. Negotiations were concluded during the summit of the European Council in December 2002. In June 2003 there was a referendum, during which the majority of Poland's citizens voted in favour of joining the European Union. On 1 May 2004 Poland and nine other countries were formally accepted as member states.

Poland voted in favour of increasing the role of the European Parliament, and for the way of voting in the European Council that had been established in Nice – a method that strengthened the position of the smaller member states, while reducing the dominance of larger nations such as Germany and France. Being a member of the European Union means that Poland can renew its old ties with western Europe.

▼ *Lech Wałęsa was awarded the Nobel Peace Prize for his work with the trade union Solidarity.*

Lech Wałęsa

Lech Wałęsa was born in 1943 to a working-class family in Popovo. He trained as an electrician and went to work in the Lenin Shipyards in Gdańsk. He made headlines in 1970 when he became the new leader of the existing trade union. In 1976, however, he was sacked because of his involvement in strikes at the shipyard. Wałęsa then co-founded a new trade union, Solidarność ('Solidarity'), but it was not acknowledged by the ruling Communist Party. In 1980, inflation saw the price of meat in Poland soar, resulting in a huge protest by the people. Strikes broke out everywhere, and Wałęsa became the spokesman for Solidarity. To end the strike, the communist government was forced to acknowledge the trade union. This caused a great deal of publicity and Wałęsa was permitted to return to his job at the shipyard. However, the economy continued to worsen and trade unions were banned. Wałęsa was arrested and briefly imprisoned. In 1983, he was awarded the Nobel Peace Prize. In 1990, Wałęsa was elected president of Poland and resigned as leader of the Solidarity movement. The years of turmoil that followed led to his defeat in the 1995 elections.

Pope John Paul II

Not even Hollywood could have made up the story of the poor Polish boy who survived two dictatorships to become one of the most influential popes in the history of the Catholic Church. Karol Wojtyla was born in the small provincial town of Wadowice on 18 May 1920, several months after Poland had regained its independence. His mother died when he was very young and he was raised by his father – a deeply religious retired army officer. Karol was very bright and was soon the top student in his school. He was also an enthusiastic athlete and showed promise as an amateur actor. However, his life was to take a very different direction. When the Second World War broke out, he was forced to put aside his academic and acting careers, and when the war ended he devoted himself to his religion. On Sunday 22 October 1978, he was solemnly ordained as Pope John Paul II in St Peter's Square in Rome. He served the Catholic people until his death in April 2005.

What can Poland offer other EU members?

Poland is not a very rich country, but it can offer agricultural products from ecologically clean areas. It can also bring its long-established culture and traditions. Poland's membership of the European Union also opens up a large market for trade and employment. The country's diverse history and geography will attract visitors from all over Europe.

What can Poland gain from EU membership?

Poland has much to gain from belonging to the EU. Among the most important are sustainable development alongside that of Europe as a whole, the opportunity to build partnerships with its neighbouring countries, and its participation in new regional alliances.

◀ *People in Poland demonstrate their support for the country becoming a member of the European Union.*

Glossary

Archbishopric The area over which an archbishop has religious control.

Communist Someone who believes that all property and industry in a country should belong to the state.

Constitution A series of laws outlining the basic principles of a government or country.

Delta A flat area at the mouth of a river, where the main river splits into smaller tributaries.

Democracy Government by officials elected by the people of a country.

Erosion The wearing away of rocks over many years by wind or water.

Middle Ages The period from around AD 500 to 1450.

NATO North Atlantic Treaty Organization; an alliance signed by a group of nations in 1949, working towards international peace and security.

Nobel Prize A series of prizes awarded every year for outstanding work in specific fields, such as Science, Medicine or Peace.

Tributary A branch of a river that flows into the main stream.

UNESCO United Nations Educational, Scientific and Cultural Organization, established to promote education and communication.

Index

Adalbertus, St 17
agriculture 12, 13, 37, 38, 39, 42, 44
air 42
architecture 4, 5, 9, 18, 19, 44, 45
Austria 7, 8
aviation 36
aurochs 44, 45
Baltic Sea 4, 10, 11, 15, 36, 45
beaches 10, 11, 44
Belarus 4
Boleslaus the Brave 17
cars 23, 35, 39, 42
Chopin, Fryderyk 25
Christmas 32, 33, 45
climate 10, 37
coal 36, 40, 42
communist regime 5, 9, 33
Copernicus, Nicolaus 25
crops 10, 37, 38
culture 6, 13, 22-25, 44
Curie, Marie 25
currency 24
Częstochowa 19
Czech Republic 4, 13
Denmark 36
dunes 10, 11, 12
Easter 32, 33, 45
education system 26-29, 43
Elbląg 12, 16, 39
emigration 8
energy 39, 42
Estonia 34
ethnic groups 23

Europe 4, 5, 7, 9, 22, 26, 34, 36, 37, 38, 46
European Union 5, 9, 25, 32, 34, 46, 47
export 36, 40
farming 12, 37, 38, 44
First World War 8
food 31-33, 37
forests 4, 11, 12, 44
France 9, 40, 46
Gdańsk 5, 15, 26, 34, 35, 36, 40, 41, 46
Germany 4, 5, 8, 9, 14, 15, 17, 18, 34, 40, 46
Giezno 17
government 24, 25
ice sheets 10
import 40
industry 5, 13, 15, 18, 20, 37, 39, 40, 41
invasion 5, 6, 9, 14, 19
Jan Sobieski III, King 14
John Paul II, Pope 5, 9, 25, 47
Katowice 18, 35, 43
kings 17, 20
Krakow 6, 7, 11, 20, 23, 35, 36, 38, 43, 45
Lake District 12, 13, 16, 17, 45
lakes 4, 10, 11, 12, 13, 43, 44
landscape 4, 10, 37, 44
language 8, 23
Latvia 34
life expectancy 23
Lithuania 4, 7, 34
livestock 37, 45

Łódź 9, 18, 36, 43
lowlands 4, 10, 34, 44
Lublin Union 7
Mazovia 14
Middle Ages 6, 7
Mieszko I, Prince 5, 6, 15, 17, 46
mountains 4, 10, 13, 21
  Carpathian 4, 13, 44
  Sudeten 5, 13, 19
  Tatra 13
national anthem 7, 24
national costume 23
national identity 5, 8
national parks 5, 11, 12, 42, 43, 44-45
NATO 25
Netherlands 12, 40
Nobel Prize 8, 9, 46
oscypek 31, 32, 38
Otto III of Germany 17
Partitions 7, 8, 24, 39
Paderewski, Ignacy 9
Piłsudski, Jósef 9
Polanski, Roman 25
pollution 41, 42, 43
population 22
Poznań 17, 23, 35
president 24, 25
Prussia 7, 8, 16
railways 34, 35
religion 5, 24
rivers 10, 11, 43, 44
  Oder 10, 11, 19, 36
  Vistula 10, 11, 12, 13, 41

roads 34, 35
Russia 4, 7, 8, 9, 34, 40
schools 26-30, 43
Second World War 5, 8, 9, 14, 15, 17, 20, 24, 39, 45, 46
shipping 35
Sienkiewicz, Henryk 8, 9
Sigismund I, King 20
Sigismund Vasa III, King 14
Slovakia 4, 13
Solidarity 9, 15, 46
Swietokrzyskie Mountains 13
tourism 13, 37, 44-45
traditions 4, 5, 8, 22
transport 5, 34-36, 40
UK 9, 40
Ukraine 4, 34
unemployment 23
UNESCO World Heritage List 20, 45
United Nations 25
universities 18, 26, 28
uplands 10, 13
Upper Silesia 13, 36, 41
USA 7, 9, 23, 36, 40
Wałęsa, Lech 46
Warsaw 8, 10, 14, 17, 25, 31, 34, 35, 36, 40, 43
water 10, 12, 42, 43
Wieliczka 20, 21
Wrocław 19, 35
Zakopane 21
Żuławy Wiślane 12, 16